MY Hands

WRITTEN BY: Destiny Moomau

About The Author:

Since graduating from Hammond High School in 2017, Destiny is a licensed Orthodontist Assistant, a postpartum doula, breastfeeding counselor, nutrition counselor and has obtained over 7 years of experience in the Early Childhood Education field. Destiny loves to play sports, read the bible and take chances in life that will make her learn new things that could impact the world in a positive way.

Dedicate this book to:

My Students:

Dani

Emmett

Jonathan

Maverick

Wensley

Janelle

Ayan

They gave me the motivation to try something new in life that would expand my love for children and reading.

Summary of 'My Hands'

This book is about a little girl who is learning the nice things she can do with her hands. She learned about sharing toys, giving her friends a high-five and praying before going to bed.

I use my hands to share fun toys with my friends.

*I use my hands to
wave them side to
side while dancing
to music.*

I use my hands to clap together to make a beat.

CLAP
CLAP

My hands are for hugging and giving people high-fives.

*I like to hold hands
with my friends.*

I use my hands to wave 'Hello' and 'Good-bye'

In the morning and
night, I use my hands
to pray to keep mean
people away.

What do you use your hands for?

www.ingramcontent.com/pod-product-compliance
Lightning Source LLC
Chambersburg PA
CBRC102038110726
48006CB00010BA/1440